INCANDESCENCE

41 POEMS - WANDERERS ARE NEVER TRULY LOST

ISHITA AND ASMIT

Dedicated to

YOU,

the over thinker

Contents

Contents

Let's Dive In

Prologue

"We are a story, yet to be discovered by a devoted reader, who'll gaze at us curiously, take us off the shelves and embrace all of our plot twists, unraveling the mysteries that lie within us."

Everyone has a story to tell, every human has their own battle to fight, their own tale to write. It may be a story of love, friendship, betrayal, life, dreams, hope, survival and so much more. It can be a story of anything and everything a person feels, jotted down. We rarely collect happy moments and rather engrave those sad parts in our lives. Sometimes you don't write your destiny, it writes you, at times, you don't choose your story, it chooses you. All you can do is strive harder, get up again if you fall. Happy moments stay in our hearts, while the sad ones in our minds and on paper. The poems you read at times may not feel relatable because every story is different, every feeling can't be explained as every human is unique in their own way. Every person has gone through something that has changed them. You can't skip the chapters of your life, you have to go through to go ahead. You'll meet different characters, weird circumstances, go on ahead, don't stop. When you cry, it doesn't mean you're a weak nobody ... It just means you've been strong for a very long time... The barrier holding up couldn't take any more and tumbled down... It doesn't mean you couldn't keep up, it means, you did well up till now! Go on love, you can still fly with broken wings. It is believed that a man is too tough to cry. The so-called toxic masculinity! Toxic masculinity is one of the most prominent manifestations of patriarchy. This belief system sees man just as a breadwinner of the family who shouldn't have any emotional vulnerabilities. Men have faced flak for expressing their emotions, but just because you're a male, doesn't mean that you're immune to human emotions. Men can cry too and it's not something to be ashamed of. You're only human, none of us are aliens now, are we? We write, to express, to relieve, to break through, to be heard and to understand ourselves. We write not to accuse but just as an excuse to tell you how it was, how it is and how everything will be from now on. Writers are people driven by the tension between the desire to speak and to hide. Stay close to anything that makes you feel alive no matter what others say, be a lover of your own world. Don't be scared to be judged by people who don't even know themselves. Societal expectations don't decide your fate or worth. Find out what your heart really wants, what is it that surges in like electricity... Understand this: you can sound confident & have anxiety at the same time... you can look healthy but feel like shit inside... You can look bubbly & be miserable inside. You'll never really understand someone unless you peek into their point of view and feel what they feel. This book is a collection of poems written over time by two people, two different lives, two different perspectives.

Here We Are

1. MI AMOR

You got a way of making me feel insane
Like I can't trust my own brain
Unless it's screaming your name
I'd have it no other way
And maybe that's why I stay
I could be somewhere, chilling on a beach
I could be with someone, making me happy
But that would be a easy love
And I don't want no easy love
I could put my phone down Just pick up my keys
I could let you go and we could let it be
But that would be too easy love
And I don't want no easy love.

2. SECRET CRUSH

~There's a thin line between love and hate. And if you switch sides, you're gonna have to play replace~

The sunlight has crawled behind those clouds
I want to put my hands on your eyes
Then ask you who I am
Meeting you has made me happy
The tree shade is on the grass
I lay with you under the cool weather
Your existence has improved my life.
The colour of the courtyard is green
That of a secret crush is orange
And in my shy eyes,
You're the prettiest colour.
How do I tell you?
I promised myself to never say it.
Even if I'm the only one who knows,
that's enough.
Meet you without an umbrella
On a dark and rainy day.
Cold, sad and fragile moments

Occupy my whole world now.
For me your blank face
Turns into a big smile.
Then I woke up from a dream
The ocean was a charming shade of blue.
I could see a ship coming from afar
That lighted up my little world.

3. I WAITED

~Let the spirit come over my soul~

I waited......I waited so long,
I waited even that day,
I waited for you to realise.
oh! there are so many
things that I can't say,
things that I can't do
only if once, if once
I would've had the courage
to proudly walk up your way
speak all I wished to say
then maybe, I guess maybe
you would've somehow accepted my flaws
accepted my honesty, accepted my heart!?
but all I can do now is ponder everyday
think about the numerous possibilities
of what we would've been if I stayed
if I wouldn't have ran away that day
what would you have said I still contemplate...

4. I SEE YOU NOW

~Caught in the haze of the moon In the brink of the lights~

A scene of you suddenly appeared
I close my eyes and I can see
A specific time and place
Sometimes I peek at you
From the shadows I
Watch you smile everyday
I wish to let you know
The feeling of sweet and sour
I'm tired of looking at you
Hiding behind the walls.

5. I'M HOPING

~Holes in my skull over time. My heart's over ice~

Hoping you know you hurt me deep
Hoping you know you made me cry
When you said you don't deserve me
And pulled it off in the middle of night
Now all my friends do is worry
They say it can be seen in my eyes
That I'm lonely and uncertain
Wondering……. If I'll ever be alright.

6. BROKEN WINGS

He made her dance in the rain
and locked her heart like a chain.
She felt like she now owned the universe
who knew it would turn out to be a curse!
His feather like touch closed her eyes
and that was when she turned blind.
She couldn't see all the stain in his lies
and the dirty games he played in her mind.
Oh my! it was late when she got aware
and then her voice was filled with despair.
Her love for him had no brakes
and now her fragile heart aches.
She thinks he was her best mistake
dear lord! her eyes can't seem to wake.
She is weeping quietly on the swing
discovering she was never his best anything!

7. STAND BY ME

~Ships go by and you wave at me~

You're so precious when you smile
I lose myself, lost in those eyes
I just had to let you know, you're mine
You're looking for god
When you're laying down your lies
I want it to be forever, even if it's time
Tell me why you still love me
When all your friends hate me.

8. SHE'S A MIRACLE

She's rare, she's kind, a poem that rhymes
she's a sunflower amidst the garden of roses
she's a beautiful shade of lavender, not gold
she's messy, confident, cute and crazy at times
she's like a butterfly, unaware of her own beauty
she's like an angel, until you push the bitch button
she dares to be different, even if she's judged
she's something to them but everything to herself
she's made up of magic and a million little dreams
she believes in her power, the sparkle in her thoughts
she knows of her ability to make people smile
she is enchanting, deep down to her very soul !!!

9. YOU WERE GOOD TO ME

~I'll make you fall in love, For a spell that can't be undone~

*Nothing's that bad if it feels too good
So you just come back like I know you would
Breathe you in till my face goes numb
Eyes closed shut while you scream out
Drop it down to that bass drum
My life without you is just numb.
I want you with me, forever
Even when we're not together
Scars imprinted in my mind so deeply
Just so I can remember
What you did to me felt like
From staring into nothingness
To never getting a wink of sleep.
Yeah.. okay.. whatever… You're right,
I'm insane But aren't you the same!?
Let me paint a small picture*

Of how it was when we were together
At least then the world can know
That words weren't enough to explain
The extravagance of those moments…
So good that it couldn't be forgotten
So bad that it couldn't be more complicated!!

10. RUNAWAY WITH ME

~The only way of love for me is 'ALL THE WAY'~

We can do anything if we put our minds to it
Take your whole life then you put a line through it
My love is yours if you're willing to take it
Give me your heart cos I ain't gonna break it
So come away with me, Starting today
Start a new life, together in a different place
We know that love is how these ideas came to be
So baby, run away Run away with me…

11. IT'S HARD TO BREATHE

~I just wanna understand~

I want to find a reason to be me
To know who I'm supposed to be.
It's tiring the process of understanding
At what place am I supposed to be standing.
It's a heart wrenching feeling
When you break more while healing.
They say I'm just a little sensitive it's nothing
I guess eventually I'll be the one I end up loathing.
I believe in myself, I really do
But sometimes it's just so very hard to
When the deep scars hurt less compared to words
I stand there shocked then stumble down afterwards.
I don't know what people think
That I'll turn into a masterpiece in a blink?
I guess originality nowadays ain't even a thing
I cant be too ambitious till the time I achieve something!

12. MY LIFE

~You found me, Gave me life~

Like water in the desert Impossible to find
you found me when I was broken
Put me back together gave me life
Like a flower in the concrete
So beautiful and rare
you gave me hope when I was empty
you're the sun to my moon.
You're my ocean painted blue
I'm nothing without you
Like an angel in a nightmare
you opened up my eyes
Looking in all the wrong places
You're the one I needed this whole time
you're the light in the dark.
You're the arrow through my heart you.
I'm nothing without you.
You're the air in my lungs
you're the veins to my blood yeah you.
I'm nothing without you

13. FIND ME

~Lost memory of the past~

I want to let you know
The feeling of sweet and sour.
I can't find a way
To prove that love is biased.
I want to give it up
But I've been fighting inwardly.
I pretend not to care
And try being busy everyday.
I can't hold myself back
Not Knowing what you're doing.
I miss you every minute
You're in my eyes all the time.
I want to control myself
Not willing to go on like this.
If this is what they call love
Then why does it feel so strange?
I don't know what to say
Maybe someday I'll find a way..

14. GALAXIES AWAY

~ The wall I built up, is faltering now ~

Waking up to nothing as
you're galaxies away from me
Watching you fall asleep at night
and lay there on my own
Got me begging for affection
All you do is roll your eyes
All my friends keep saying that
I'm way too good to you
But my heart is so invested,
I don't wanna face the truth
I'm not happy and you know it
and you still don't even try
Broken down, I've had enough
If this is love I don't want it now.

15. WHY DO WE PONDER

~I tried so hard, but it's still too dark~

I've been thinking about my ex lately
About the person that she made me
The person I wasn't, I've become
I've been trying to fill this empty void
But, I feel more empty than I did
Now, I could really use some love
Trying to find a reason to get up
Been trying to find a reason for this stuff
All the skeletons in my closet, and
The baggage in my heart is still so dark

16. THE UNTOLD - SHE

~Sometimes, we value those who don't actually care about us~

Little do you know
How bad I'm hurting everyday
You said you'll never leave,
Yet you walked away
You said you loved me,
Yet you abandoned me
You said you cared,
Yet you camouflaged your thoughts
You said I'm pretty,
Yet you called me ugly
You said you'll never break me,
Yet you broke me first
You said you were happy,
Yet found happiness elsewhere
You said my voice is your favourite tune,
Yet you covered your ears

ISHITA AND ASMIT

You said my heart's pure,
Yet you left it shattered
You said you're always here.
Yet you're now a stranger
You said you think of me
Whenever the moon rises
Yet I'm alone right here
Now when the rain pours!!

17. THE UNTOLD - HE

*~Sometimes, we value those who don't actually care
about us~*

Little do you know
I know what I did was erroneous
I'm sorry that I lied to you
I'm sorry I fooled you from the start
I'm sorry you thought I loved you
I'm sorry that I never did
I'm sorry I can't turn back time
I'm sorry for breaking your heart
I'm sorry for making you cry all night
I'm sorry I hurt you even though you're sweet
I'm sorry I made promises I couldn't keep
No amount of I'm sorry's can mend things up
But I'm sorry for every bad thing I did
I hope you forgive me someday
I hope you find that someone
He who will help you move on
He who tells you you're worth everything
He who never judges your cute childish self

He who bandages your broken soul
He who loves you more than himself
He who's not like me, but someone better.

18. LET THEM GO

~You'll heal, you'll move on, eventually~

I never meant to be a problem
I never meant to cause you pain
I didn't want to break it up
But there wasn't another way.
You're not the only one who's hurting
Not the only one with scars
But now you gotta admit
That we were drifting apart.
We'll feel broken for sometime
But you'll find the strength
To walk again when you're weak.
You'll fight against your heavy heart
And find love blooming slowly inside
When you least expect it
It could be any minute now.
Don't fight the tears rolling down
It's lighter after you let them go
Then why have I been crying over you
For the life of me, I wish that I knew.

19. TO BE HEARD

~Sometimes, It's okay to not be okay~

It breaks me everytime I realise
That all I do is nothing in your eyes.
You give me everything I wish for
But I fail to give you what you wish of.
You just don't see how hard I tried
I know I'm not that perfect someone
But an imperfectly perfect self.
I'm different, weird, messy
And maybe a tad bit crazy.

20. THE PAIN YOU GIVE

~IF ONLY LOVING YOU WAS JUST LOVING UNCONDITIONALLY, IF ONLY IT CAME WITHOUT SUCH PAIN, IF ONLY IT CAME WITHOUT ANY HINDRANCES.. I WONDER HOW LIFE WOULD'VE BEEN~

I tried to reach you, cos I can't hide
How strong's the feeling when we dive
I crossed the dark ocean of my mind
My wounds are now healing with time
All my senses are now intensified
Oh girl! Whenever we dive
I cross the ocean of my mind
But in the end it's me who dies
You drag me down to drown alone
That's what you do, my girl!

21. CAN YOU HEAR ME

you don't get me, you never did
and you don't give a damn about it.
all the time you praise someone else
like they're the only ones you ever see.
all the time you say I'm worthless
cos I am not what you wanted me to be.
how is it you never noticed
that you were slowly killing me!

22. LOST, I AM

Talking to myself
wishing for your presence right now
Craving for you to hold me down
And catch my tears right now
Cos I'm lonely knowing that only you
could heal my frown right now
It's true, it's only you nobody else I ask for

23. STAND UP AGAIN

~Bit by bit, brick by brick, build yourself again~

the ice keeps on melting
the fire keeps on raging
the water keeps on rolling
the heart keeps on flowing
the age keeps on growing
the smile keeps on fading
but even after all this
my tears keep on flowing

24. AN EMOTION

~Black is not a colour but an emotion~

Every time we meet,
Everything is sweet.
Oh, you're so tender,
I must surrender
You're the one I long to kiss
Baby, you're the one I really miss
You're the one I'm dreaming of
Baby, you're the only one I love
Keep me in your heart,
Never let us part
Ooh, never leave me,
Don't ever deceive me
My love is your love,
Now and forever
You're the one I want,
You must believe me.

25. IT'S TIME NOW

*~It is not tragic, If you lost someone, But found
yourself~*

You say that time can't heal
the broken heart you stole
You are something I can't feel
can't understand what is real
Oh, this something in my heart
makes me miss you more.

26. EXPECTATIONS

~Disappointment is only when you expect~

My vision is blurring now
All my aspirations crashing down
I've never felt this way before
All of what was left of me died
I can see the sun rising
Melodies and colours capture the sky.

27. GO THROUGH

~Go through the darkest of days~

It's been hard to open up
cos when I lost you
I lost my belief in trust
I was scared knowing that
anyone and everyone could
leave me in the dust
when all of it fell down,
that's when it required
for me to look up.
but now I'm stuck wondering
why on earth we can't
just rewind that day
it was you, the first girl
I ever truly loved
but then, you still made
my damn heart hurt!

28. STAY

~The problem is, we think we have time~

When you try your best
but you don't succeed
When you're smiling outside
but suffocating beneath
When it hurts so much
but you gotta go on.
When it doesn't affect you
but your heart does bleed
When they think you don't care
but you're breaking beneath
When they say you're worthless
but you try not to believe.
When you're tryna move on
but you have chains on your feet
When you're struggling climbing up
but still stumbling downwards
When your ears are ringing hard
but you gotta be strong
When it hurts so freaking much

but can only clench your teeth
When you've had too much
but can only bite your inner cheek
When it burns you from within
but gotta hold back your tears.

29. AS IT WAS

Voices, thoughts and memories
Remind me of those merry days
When I used to be so carefree
Dancing to some old melody
And singing to my own tunes.
Look where we are standing now
Look at what we're doing
Look at how everything changed
Look at how we've grown.
We used to be crazy little kids
Now we're nothing more or less
Than broken pieces of a mug
Gluing together our life, bit by bit.
The sand castles we used to make
The doors have trapped us in today
Oh, how loved we were those days
Now, we're not worth more than grades.
Our struggles, no one cares of
Our thoughts are merely excuses

Our happiness is something forgotten
Our lives are no longer ours to judge.
We're now the talk of the town
How we couldn't wear a crown
How we weren't brilliant and sound
How we were a big burden around.
This is not my story, but of every human
Struggling to make something of their lives
Living, Caring, breaking and always hurt
An invisible rope tightening their breaths.
The Adults are trying to web together
The pieces of their shattered lives and dreams
The kid in them is struggling to break free
To live life as it earlier used to be, sweet.

30. A VIBE

~Soulmates is not just a word, it's a vibe~

Hey! it's raining cats and dogs here
What about where you are?
Is it pouring down or is it hot around?
Is it chilly or a randomly pleasant feeling?
You must be laughing right... at me?
probably thinking about my stupidity
what am i doing, wondering about you
when i should be enjoying the breeze...
but what can i do now than just ponder
when every droplet reminds me of you!!

31. DREAM ON

~Dreaming is never too costly~

Sometimes I wonder......
am I afraid of thunder?
or is it the lightning?
that seems a bit frightening.
Walking with this weird feeling,
when nothing seems ethical.
They say it's nothing else,
I'm just depressed
ever had a hunch....
that I might be suppressed?

32. KEEP HER SAFE

~She's delicate as a feather, strong as iron~

Sensitive to despair
Hearkens to others welfare
Delicate, she's elsewhere
Beautiful, beyond compare
If you meet her, best beware
She'll steal your heart unaware
She's me, I am her, the very girl
There's no one like her anymore
She'll mesmerize you, I swear
Don't go after her, she's fragile
Look after her, just for a while.

33. I TRIED SO HARD

~It wasn't just about trying~

I tried, you did too
But I guess it never was
About trying our very best.
Because that was not all
Required for us to run away.
It required hope and belief
A little extra strength in me.
To runaway to someplace
Where no one comes to thee.
With sorry excuses and hurt
With judging eyes and heart.
Let's runaway, you and me
To some place where we
Can be 'we', not how they
Wish for us to actually be..

34. BREAK THROUGH

~Grow through what you go through~

Heyy!! I'll be narrating a story today
You, in the crowd, better listen to me
It's very interesting, I promise.
Once upon a time, it goes
There once was this person
Living someone else's dream.
Trying to be that human
She was never meant to be.
She was quiet from the start
Never paid heed to her heart.
Wishing to be from a fairytale
Waiting to be pulled out.
She wanted people to understand
How her life's not roses and stars.
How she's struggling too, you know
To make her mark in this world.
You, in the crowd, listen and realise
It's your life, spelt out of my mouth.
Someone finally found the keys

To the secret diary you forever hid.
The sorrows you stored were a lot
Happy moments were never a part.
I found the memories you stored
The story you wished to be known.
It's your story, come out here love
Pick up that pen and rewrite your heart.
Change what is supposed to happen
Change your negative thoughts.
Now that your story is heard,
Would your life be different, or not.
Would it shock you the most to see
You are not who they thought you to be.
The things that earlier defined you
Can now be summed up in three words.
I'm glad your story was heard this time
Move on, make a better life for yourself.
You ask how I know all these so much
Well it wasn't just your dream to be heard.
To be understood without any explanation
To be believed in, trusted and talked about.

35. YOU BROKE ME FIRST

~It 's hard to breathe, but I'll be fine~

Not all mistakes can be forgiven with a sorry
Not all things can be weighed down with a thanks
Not all selfless acts can be understood by others
Not all pain from betrayals can be explained aptly
Being selfless, lead me down a dark dark alley
Caring for you, made me crash into a bitter reality
A place I never imagined I'd find myself standing
Yet, I stood there, trying to erase every little memory
I still behaved like I used to do, all smiley, jolly
But from inside I stopped believing in you
I died a little every time I saw you happily pass by
Carefree, confident and totally unaware, that I knew
I knew what you did to me that summer, I knew it then
September ain't just a month and 2018 just a year
But the time frame, my life was inches away from hell
I did stupid things for you, you never knew, well how would
you?

I blindly devoted my heart for you, I lied for the first time
To every single person, just for you, my friend
I was acting all along, but you never even noticed
Actually, how would you? You never cared like I did
I was there just to be used, I knew, but I kept quiet
For everything I did went down the drain that day
The moment you decided you couldn't just sit idle
And that my happiness was not worth the wait
Just forget and forgive, you can't dwell on it forever
Yeah, okay, if you say so, I'll forgive but I can't forget
I don't remember much, but it's still in there, buried
In some part of my heart that can't be vacuumed
I'm better than you, have always been, it's proved
This is just the beginning of the story, yet it's long
I'll tell you the rest of it someday again, today, I can't
Because my eyes are now blurred by blank emotions
Tears have resurfaced as the recollections flash by
I will complete this sob story once I bury them back
Once I'm done trying to forget for the umpteenth time
I'm not that weak, I'll be fine again, as I always am.

36. INTRODUCING HIM

~A summary of who he used to be and who he is now~

I have a friend who once was an enemy
He is now who he didn't used to be, altruistic.
He thinks, no he strongly believes that
If someone's gonna get hurt, it should be me.
He's afraid of hurting everyone but himself
One day, he shares with me a story
Then at the end asks me if he can trust me?
He already does, but has been hurt very much
And confirmations do console now don't they?
He thinks it doesn't matter if he's the one who cries
It doesn't matter even if he dies crying.
It doesn't matter how deep he's burying himself
It doesn't matter if in future he can be pulled out.
He thinks… now that he's become selfless
He can't say no, he can't put himself first.
How very charming but naïve he is

If he can't put himself first and love himself..
How does he intend to care for others
When he can't even think of himself.
I tried being his therapist, a true friend
I did all I could till the end…
But what can I do now if he doesn't listen
Other than hoping it all ends well.
He overthinks, afraid of how
Every little thing he says may look like.
How everything he does may sound like
And now, even if it hurts, he'll go along .
He'll go along till the day it's too late
Too late to think what if I chose the other road that day…

37. MY MIND

~the mind is adamant to stay~

I sat down quietly today
Doing nothing in particular
Trying to calmly figure out
Which way I'm actually headed.
In fact I got a few answers
Noy exactly to the big question
But to a million little ones
That were hiding in a corner.
It doesn't need to make sense
It doesn't need to be all laid out
Going with the flow, the beats
Is better than memorizing the rhythm.
Today wasn't much of a fruitful day
But I felt serene, I felt confident
Like there still was, sorry, Is HOPE
I can prove that I'm capable enough!

38. FLAWED BELIEFS

*~Be proud of who you are, not who you're supposed
to be~*

IF I'M PRETTY
You'll talk about me behind my back
IF I'M UGLY
you would hesitate to talk to me at all
IF I DRESS SHORT
You'll call me an attention seeker
IF I DRESS PROPERLY
you'll say it's to hide my chubby thighs
IF I CRY
You'll say I'm emotionally unstable
IF I DON'T
you'll say I ain't a bit sensitive
IF I'M AN EXTROVERT
you'll call me clingy and talkative
IF I'M AN INTROVERT
you'll say I'm conservative and shy
IF I CARE
you'll think I'm interested in you

IF I DON'T
you'll say i have an attitude problem
IF I TALK TO BOYS
you'll call me needy or maybe a whore
IF I TALK LESS OR DON'T
you'll say I'm a silent killer and not a chirpy soul
IF I SHARE MY SECRETS
You'll say I trust people too easily
IF I HESITATE OR DON'T
you'll say I don't trust people at all
IF I LIE ABOUT STUFF
You'll say it improves my image, I'll look cool
IF I DON'T
you'll say I'm not sweet, but a big fool
IF I GO HOME EARLY
you'll call me boring, a party pooper
IF I GO HOME LATE
You'll call me oh so outgoing, a slut
IF I HAVE ZERO FIGURE
You'll say Is she even a girl? What a bore
IF I'M PLUMPY
you'll comment on the so called assets I own
IF I USE HARSH WORDS
You'll call me a part of the cool group
IF I REFRAIN
you'll say I'm a part of the three year olds
IF I'M GOOD AT A LOT OF STUFF

ISHITA AND ASMIT

You'll call me a freak, a robot
IF I'M NOT
you'll say I'm incapable, a Dumbo.

• 51 •

39. OVERTHINKING

~her heart's ready to break down now~

I'm a professional overthinker
But sometimes I find peace
I know loving you hurts me
But leaving you breaks me.
I know I'll miss you if I leave
But then again staying cuts deep
I was silent, not blind you see
A smile can hide so much pain.
Maybe I don't ever say much
But remember I do feel it
It hurts, but I'll just hide it
I lied when I said I was fine.
Just remember this one thing
If I especially come and ask about it
I know about it, so don't lie please
I lost a little if measured, found a lot.
i ran and ran and ran, endlessly
But I guess there ain't an end to it
I think I'll be sad forever inside

While smiling brighter outside
A lot of feelings for one person
To all of those broken souls out there
You're heard
You're understood
Your pain can be felt
You deserve so much more
"Forget the ones who forget you"
I hate how tiny things hurt a lot
Sometimes I can't tell what I feel
I want me back, cos this isn't me.

40. LIGHT, WHEN IT'S DARK

From those rusty brown windows
Seeps through a dusty yellow light
She feels a fuzzy -warming feeling
A ray of hope bubbling inside.
She is forever stuck in that catacomb
Completely unaware of the ways of life
Her world revolves in a small dark room
And not some fancy palace of night.
Humming an in incoherent tune, she lives
Gazing those walls, one day, she dies
If, If only she wasn't left behind
Maybe shell be dancing in halls to night.
She's stuck in there forever, she's aware
Weaving those cobwebs into a curtain
To block those rays coming from outside
Giving her a false hope, that she'll survive.
Break the silence, the walls around

Hold on to the hope seeping inside
You'll be free one day, you'll be fine
You're a warrior girl, you'll survive.

41. RAISON D'ETRE

~I need you to hold on~

Can you hear me?
Dealing with my own mayhem.
Can you hear me?
I'm trying to express myself.

⁓

My vision is blurring now
All my aspirations crashing down.
It's an uncanny feeling, cause
I'm drowning while healing.
It breaks me every time I realize
I'm never gonna be good enough.

⁓

Think of it just once
If you ever heard my screams.
My muffled cries at night
Weren't the prettiest sight.
They don't get me, never did
And that was slowly killing me.

⁓

I can see both, emptiness and hope
One reminding me to depart, I've lost enough.
One stringing me to hold on, live afresh
I know it's up to me, every little thing.
To create a desert void of life and happiness
Or make the summer spring.

~

What if I choose the glass that's only half filled
Drain it and fill it up all over again.
Only with dreams, hope, hard work
And courage, one drop at a time..
Start afresh, strive harder, get back up
Try, it's the least you could do for yourself.

~

Can you hear me?
I'm trying to be someone else.
Can you hear me?
I'm often talking to myself.

~

When you try your best, but don't succeed
When it doesn't affect you, but your heart does bleed
When the deep scars hurt less compared to words
When they say you're worthless, but you try not to believe
When it burns you from within and you bite your inner cheek
I ask of you, keep going, if you fall, get up again, for yourself.

~

INCANDESCENCE

I want to find a reason to be me
To know who I'm supposed to be.
It's tiring, the process of understanding
At what place am I supposed to be standing.
I believe in myself, but at times it's hard to continue
I guess eventually I'll be the one I end up loathing.

Sometimes I wonder, am I afraid of thunder?
Or is it the lightening that seems a bit frightening.
They don't know my carefree attitude is just a façade
Hiding my suffocations, things that always haunt me.
Walking ahead with this weird heavy feeling
When nothing around me seems ethical.

They say, it's nothing much, I'm just depressed
Ever had a hunch, that I might be suppressed?
All they do is compare; all you do is overthink
But no one ever said, between studying and living
CHEERS! To growing, believing and going on ahead…
CHEERS! You did it, you survived and it actually matters.

Can you hear me?
I'm screaming in my head.
Can you hear me?
At times I wish I was dead.

But, there came a day, I saw a hopeful ray
I found solace in places I never knew existed.
I found a bright light, that made me smile wide
People, who were grateful for my mere existence.
Musicians that comforted me, music that lingered
It's true, the right people will make you love yourself too.

~

I'm not putting up filters, a façade, not anymore
Cause people will forever doubt the purity of gold.
Now I know, I never was less worthy of anything
I was just a yellow sunflower in the garden of roses.
It took me longer to realise, I hope you'll start now
My life's worth living, and I'm stronger than before.
Fly like a butterfly, take your light along like a firefly!

~

Can you hear me?
I'm giggling, achieving, believing
Can you hear me?
I'm not scared or hurt anymore
I actually came out of that dark hole…

THANK YOU

A chapter ends, another begins

<u>*If you liked our poems, support us by sharing this book with others!! Also available as an ebook on Kindle and Notionpress.*</u>

~

<u>***For more updates, follow us***</u>

<u>***on INSTAGRAM***</u>

<u>***@dazed.words***</u>

Until Next Time